17 More Prehistoric Monsters

EVERYONE SHOULD KNOW ABOUT

STANTON F. FINK

VOLUME XII OF STANTON'S COLORING BOOKS

Acknowledgments

and Dedication

To my father, in whose books I discovered my first monsters.

To Will Caligan, whose help and encouragement is one of the primary reasons for this coloring book's existence.

To Mariano Silvera, who should have had his own artbooks

To Doctor David Morafka, who helped teach me to be more picky with my information.

To my friends, who helped push me to make this.

Table of Contents

Introduction

The purpose of this coloring book series is to provide information on various prehistoric animals both profoundly famous and incredibly obscure to artists of all ages. Of course, there is a lot of material to work with, as animals have been a major component of Earth's ecosystems for at least 670 million years.

For the sake of space and workability, each volume will contain 17 entries: ideally, one species for each geological time period, if possible. If you, or your inner and or outer child do not see your favorite prehistoric animal here, it may be eventually featured in another volume. Or, contact me to have it put into a later volume.

Glossary

- **Aquatic**- Living in water.
- **Arthropod**- Any member of the animal phylum Arthropoda, including trilobites, arachnids, crustaceans, insects, myriapods and their relatives. All arthropods have armor-like, jointed exoskeletons made of chitin-derived plates, sometimes reinforced with calcium carbonate, and jointed limbs.
- **Cambrian**- A period of time in the Paleozoic Era from 541 to 485 million years ago.
- **Carboniferous**- A period of time in the Paleozoic Era from 359 to 300 million years ago.
- **Cenozoic**- An era of time in the Phanerozoic Eon from 65 million years ago until now.
- **Chordate**- Any member of the animal phylum Chordata, including sea squirts, lancet fish, and vertebrates (such as lampreys, sharks, tuna, frogs, lizards, chickens, and people). All chordates have, at least at some point in their life cycle, a notochord, a long, flexible rod, usually made of cartilage, or, in the case of most vertebrates, cartilage and bone, running down the back from head to tail, directly beneath the neural tube.
- **Cnidarian**- Any member of the animal phylum Cnidaria, such as jellyfish, box jellies, Portuguese Man'o'war, sea anemones, coral and the parasitic myxozoans. Cnidarians are usually radially symmetrical, and have unique, venom-injecting stinging cells called "cnidocytes."
- **Cretaceous**- The last period of time in the Mesozoic Era, from 144 to 66 million years ago.
- **Devonian**- A period of time in the Paleozoic Era from 414 to 360 million years ago.
- **Ediacaran**- The last period of time in the Precambrian Eon from 635 to 542 million years ago.
- **Eocene**- A period of time in the Cenozoic Era from 55 to 33 million years ago.
- **Fauna**- In an ecological context, "fauna" refers to the animal components of an ecosystem.
- **Formation**- In a geological or paleontological context, a formation is a group of rock layers.
- **Gnathostome**- A gnathostome is any vertebrate chordate with a moveable jaw (or had an ancestor with one).
- **Holocene**- A period of time in the Cenozoic Era from 12,000 years ago until now.
- ***Incertae sedis***- A Latin phrase literally meaning "uncertain seat." *"Incertae sedis"* is a term in classification used to refer to a species or group whose relationships with related organisms are unclear or poorly defined.
- **Jurassic**- The second period of time in the Mesozoic Era, from 199 to 145 million years ago.
- **Mesozoic**- An era of time in the Phanerozoic Eon from 249 to 66 million years ago.
- **Miocene**- A period of time in the Cenozoic Era from 23 to 5 million years ago.

- **Mollusk**- Any member of the animal phylum Mollusca, including snails, clams, squid, octopuses, tusk shells and chitons. Most mollusks have a calcium carbonate shell, and a toothed, file-like tongue called a radula. All mollusks have a cape-like organ, the mantle, which usually secretes the shell, and houses breathing organs, and a nervous system.
- **Nekton**- Any aquatic animal that lives either entirely or almost entirely in the water column, and relies on its own swimming or propulsion abilities to keep and move itself in and around the water column. Anchovies, porpoises and ichthyosaurs are examples of nekton.
- **Neogene**- The second third of the Cenozoic Era, comprising of the Miocene and the Pliocene periods.
- **Oligocene**- A period of time in the Cenozoic Era from 33 to 23 million years ago.
- **Ordovician**- A period of time in the Paleozoic Era from 484 to 440 million years ago.
- **Paleocene**- A period of time in the Cenozoic Era from 65 to 55 million years ago.
- **Paleogene**- The first third of the Cenozoic Era, comprising of the Paleocene, Eocene, and Oligocene.
- **Paleozoic-** An era of time in the Phanerozoic Eon from 249 to 66 million years ago.
- **Permian**- The last period of time in the Paleozoic Era, the time of "The Great Dying," or most severe of all known extinction events, from 299 to 250 million years ago.
- **Pharynx**- A structure in the throat of many animals located directly behind the mouth or oral chamber. In vertebrates, it often houses breathing structures, like gills.
- **Plankton**- An organism that uses water currents and waterflow to as its primary means of transportation in the water column because it is either too small to move long distances by its own power, or lacks the ability to propel itself entirely. Sargassum seaweed and jellyfish are two varieties of plankton.
- **Pleistocene**- A period of time in the Cenozoic Era from 3 million years ago until 12 thousand years ago.
- **Pliocene**- A period of time in the Cenozoic Era from 5 to 3 million years ago.
- **Quaternary**- The last third of the Cenozoic Era, comprising of the Pleistocene and the Holocene periods.
- **Terrestrial**- Living on land.
- **Triassic**- The first period of time in the Mesozoic Era, from 249 to 200 million years ago.

Name

Moose Proarticulatan

Species   *Lossinia lissetskii*

Phylum   Proarticulata

Class   *incertae sedis*

Size   Length 3 to 8 milimeters, width 2 to 5 milimeters

Time Period   Late Ediacaran of the Precambrian, 555 million years ago

Location   Verkhovka and Yorga Formations, Winter Coast ("Zimnii Bereg") of the Arkhangelsk Region of the White Sea, Russia.

Comments   The Moose Proarticulatan, *Lossinia lissetskii*, is named after the Losinoe ("Moose") Bog near where the first fossils were originally found, in Russia, on the Winter Coast of the White Sea.

The moose proarticulatan is peculiar even by proarticulatan standards, which says a lot, actually. While it demonstrates the characteristic staggered symmetry of the group, its arrangement of its isomers as cute, little limb-like extensions of the main body is unique. This arrangement does, however, recall the isomer arrangements of other "oddball" proarticulatans, like *Onega*, *Armillifera*, or the cattle brand proarticulatan, *Tamga hamulifera*, shown here with the moose proarticulatan.

The moose proarticulatan's lifestyle would probably be identical to its relatives, externally digesting and absorbing biofilms along the seafloor when not scuttling around on microscopic cilia. So far, though, its feeding traces have not been found.

Name — Maotianshan Skelejelly

Species	*Maotianoascus octonarius*
Phylum	Ctenophora
Class	Scleroctenophora
Family	Vetulicolidae
Size	About 1.5 centimeters in length, 1 centimeter in diameter.
Time Period	"Stage 3" of the Cambrian Period, 515 million years ago
Location	Maotianshan section of Chengjiang County, and Sanjiezi section of Jinning, Yunnan Province, China
Comments	The Maotianshan Skelejelly, *Maotianoascus octonarius*, is one of six known (five of which are officially described) species of scleroctenophoran combjellies. Scleroctenophoran combjellies are easily distinguished from other combjellies by the presence of eight internal ribs radiating from the statocyst (a jewel-shaped blister at the top of the animal that aids in orientating itself while swimming), so that the living animal would have looked like a swimming, carnivorous lampshade. So far, all of them are restricted to the Maotianshan or Chengjiang Fauna of Chengjiang County, of Lower Cambrian Yunnan Province. The Maotianshan skelejelly is the first combjelly found in the Chengjiang Fauna, though, its identity as a scleroctenophoran was not determined until fossils of more combjellies were found during the 2010's that showed the internal skeletons more clearly. *M. octonarius*' eight ribs formed eight lobes arranged in a globular shape, and it had a large, skirt-like mouth. Here, it is the largest of three Chengjiang combjellies, the others being *Batofasciculus* (the 2nd largest), and *Sinoascus* (the smallest).

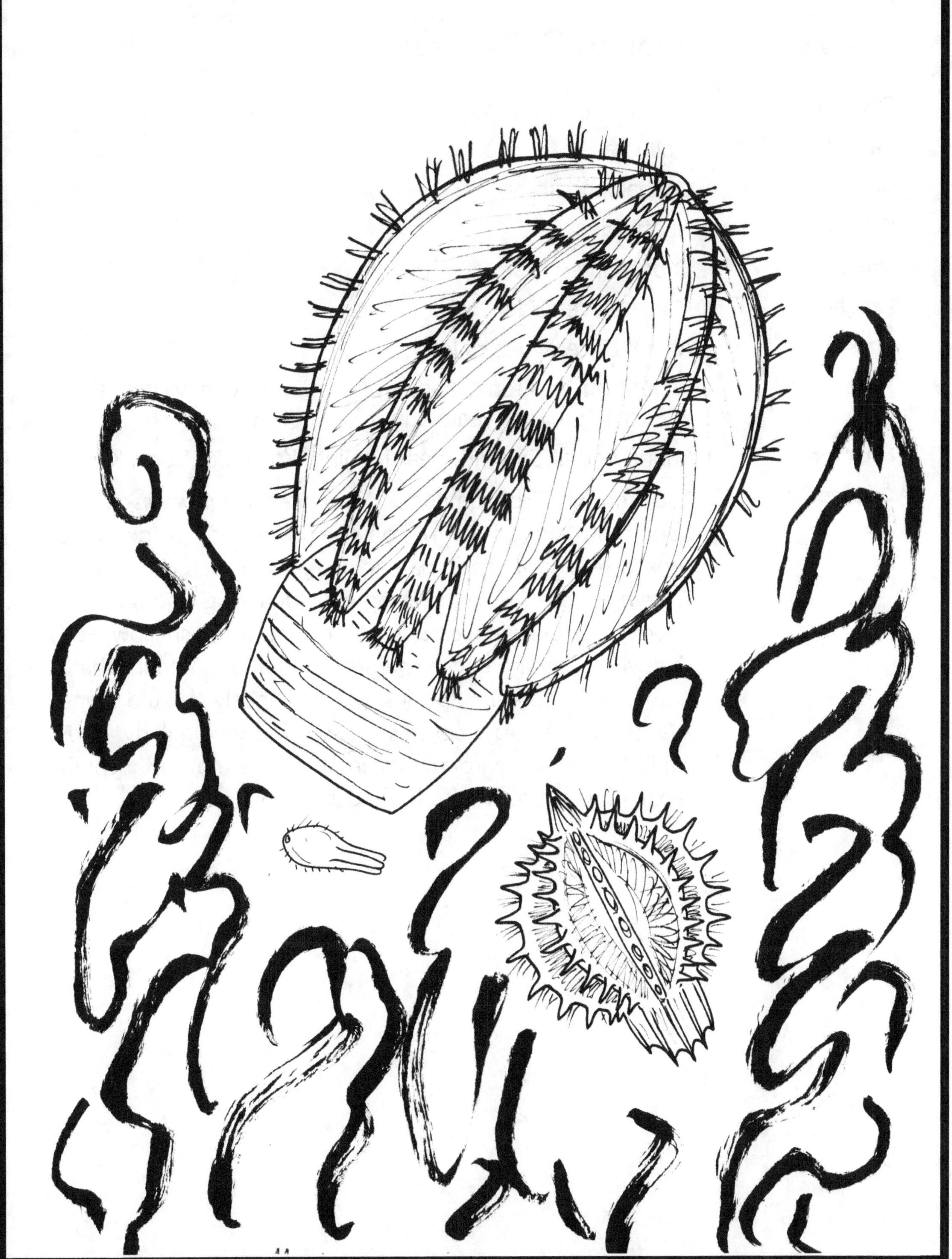

Name Shorinri Croissantilus

Species	*Coreanoceras shorinense*
Phylum	Mollusca
Class	Cephalopoda
Subclass	Nautiloidea
Order	Endocerida
Family	Manchuroceratidae
Size	About 10 centimeters long
Time Period	Wolungian or Arenig Epoch of the Early Ordovician, about 478 to 472 million years ago
Location	Shorin Bed at Shorinri, near Kenjiho, Kokai-do, North Korea
Comments	The Shorinri Croissantilus, *Coreanoceras shorinense*, is an abberrant, curved ("cyrtoconic") species of a genus of otherwise cigar-shaped nautiloids (i.e., compare the shell of *C. kemipoense* below the living individual of *C. shorinense*). Species of *Coreanoceras* were restricted to shallow Early Ordovician marine environments in the Shorin Bed in what is now North Korea. Species of the closely related genus *Manchuroceras*, by contrast, were found similarly aged, similar marine environments in what are now Manchuria, Japan, China, North America and Tasmania.

Name

(Heinz Christian) Pander's Hexautilus

Species	*Hexameroceras panderi*
Phylum	Mollusca
Class	Cephalopoda
Order	Oncocerida
Family	Hemiphragmoceratidae
Size	Shell up to 8 centimeters in length
Time Period	Late Ludlow epoch of the Middle Silurian, 423 million years ago
Location	Bohemia, Czech Republic

Comments

The (Heinz Christian) Pander's Hexautilus, *Hexameroceras panderi*, is one of several teardrop-shaped ("breviconic") nautiloid cephalopods from Silurian-aged marine environments of what is now Bohemia. Related species of hexautilii are found in Late Silurian-aged marine environments in Western Europe and Eastern North America, as well.

Pander's hexautilus was not a fast or efficient swimmer, and probably either ate plankton, or captured nektonic prey. The opening of the shell is sculpted to have three pairs of connected slots, possibly for the eyes and tentacles, and a seventh slot for the siphon to extrude from.

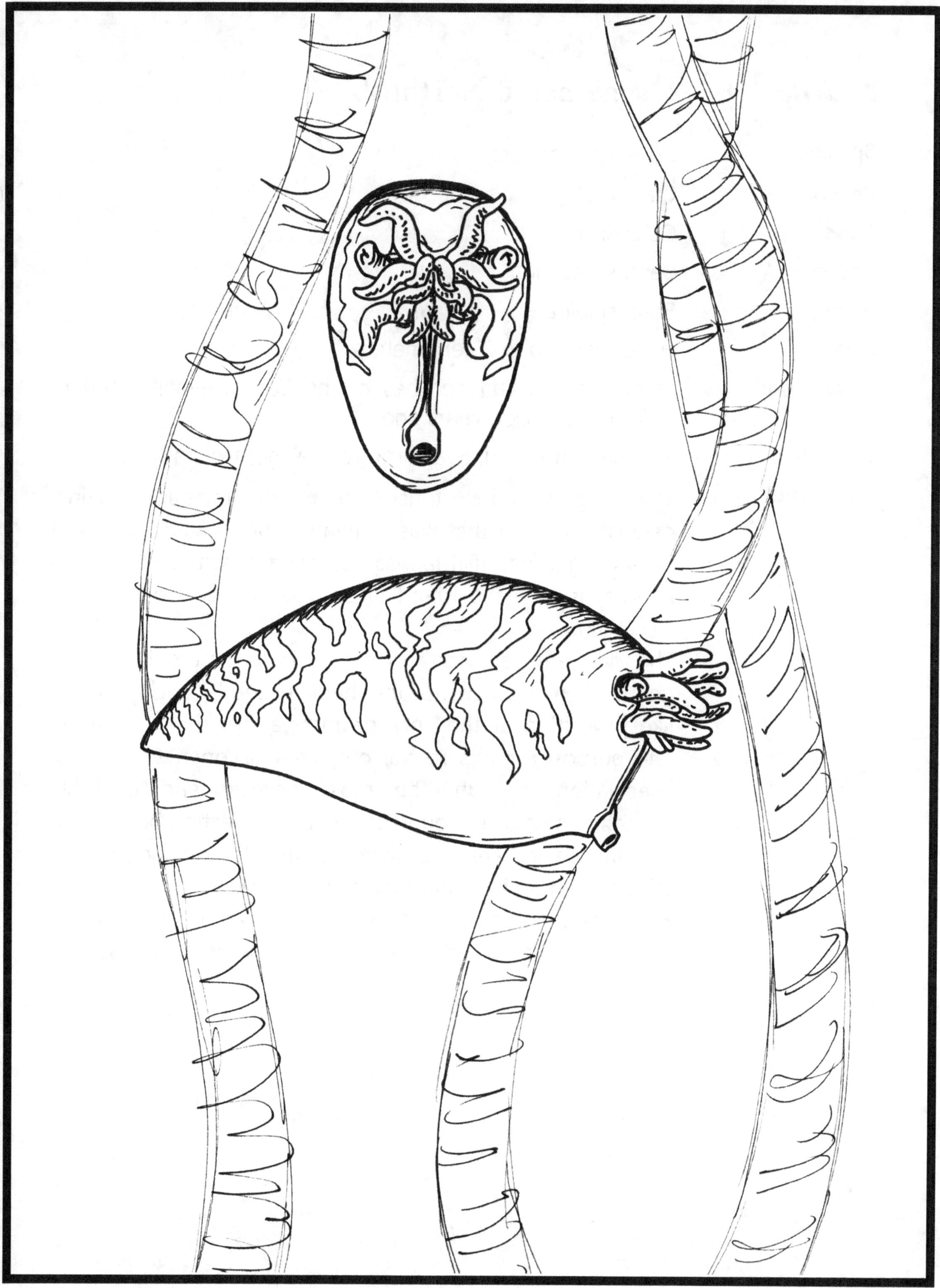

Name   Daggernosed Northfish

Species	*Boreaspis rostrata*
Phylum	Chordata
Class	Osteostraci
Order	Benneviaspidida
Family	Boreaspididae
Size	Headshield up to 2 centimeters
Time Period	Pragian to Emsian epoches of the Early Devonian period, 410 to 400 million years ago
Location	Spitzbergen Island, Svalbard Archipelago, Norway

Comments

The Daggernosed Northfish, *Boreaspis rostrata*, is an extinct osteostracan fish that was a member of a diverse series of diverse agnathan fish faunas that lived in saltwater lagoons in what is now the island of Spitzbergen during the Early Devonian.

The daggernosed northfish's genus, *Boreaspis,* is a large genus of small osteostracans characterized by a long, spine-like projection at the anteriormost-part of the headshield. The purpose of this rostral projection is open to a lot of speculation, though, the most popular and plausible hypotheses revolve around the rostral projection being used to enhance the animal's hydrodynamics and being used to stir up the mud in its hunt for edible particles to eat.

Here, the daggernosed northfish is compared with its much, much larger relative, the meteorfish, *Parameteoraspis sp.*

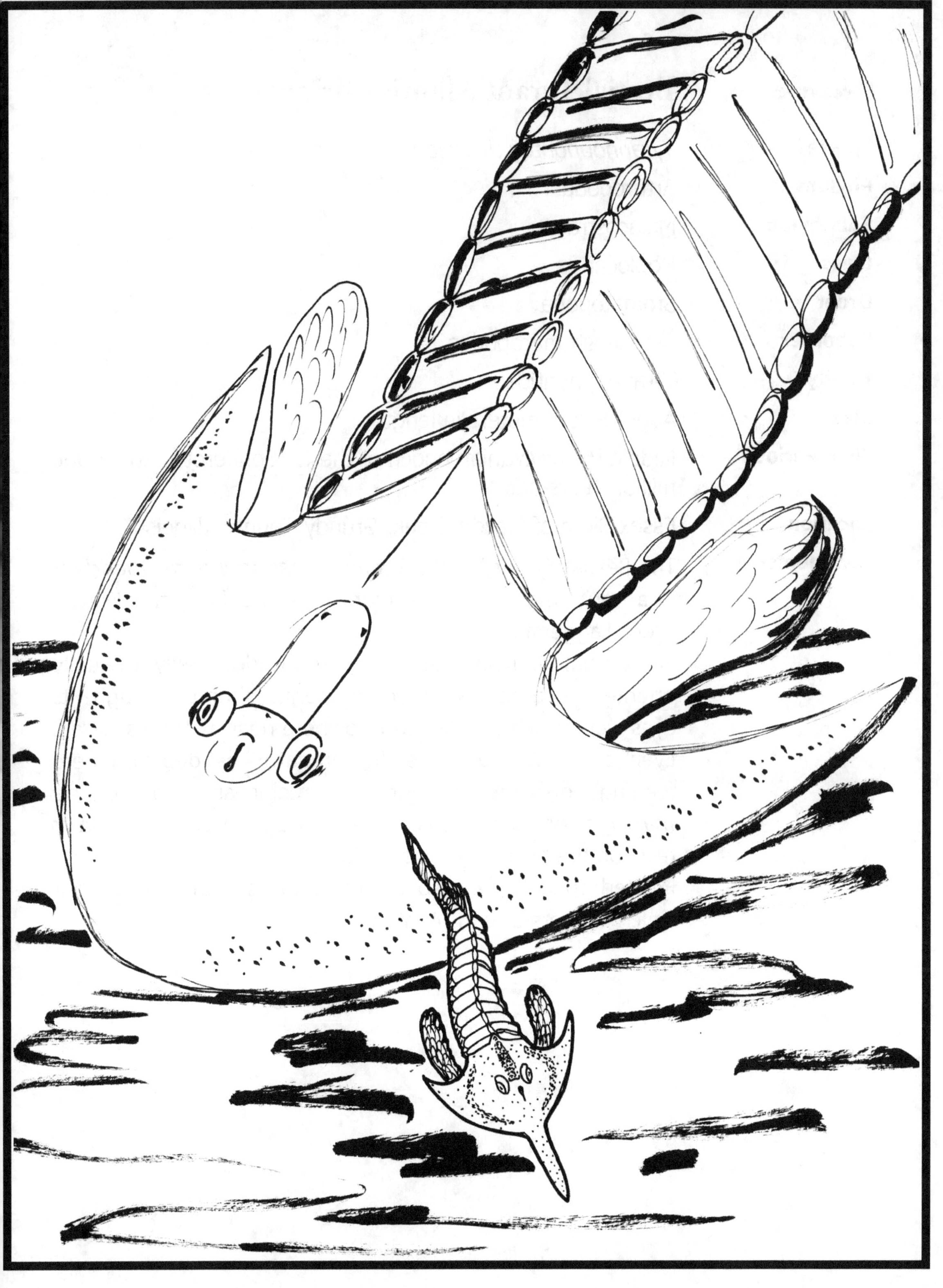

Name

Bestial Tyrant Mantis Shrimp

Species	*Tyrannophontes theridion*
Phylum	Arthropoda
Subphylum	Malacostraca
Class	Hoplocarida
Order	Stomatopoda
Suborder	Archaeostomatopodea
Family	Tyrannophontidae
Size	About 5 centimeters in length
Time Period	Middle Pennsylvanian epoch of the Carboniferous, about 300 million years ago
Location	Essex Biota of Mazon Creek, Grundy County, Illinois

Comments

The Bestial Tyrant Mantis Shrimp, *Tyrannophontes theridion*, is a very small, primitive mantis shrimp from the Mazon Creek Laggerstätte.

The bestial tyrant mantis shrimp was undoubtedly a visually oriented predator like modern mantis shrimp, though, its eyes were much smaller, and nowhere near as sophisticated. Even so, it was a successful predator, as depicted here feeding on the phyllocarid crustacean *Kellibrooksia macrogaster* (the hemicaridean *Eucryptocaris asherorum* rests on the bestial tyrant's back).

Related species are also found in the similarly aged Bear Gulch Laggerstätte in Montana.

Name   Sponge Lily

Species   *Calceolispongia hindei*

Phylum   Echinodermata

Class   Crinoidea

Subclass   Camerata

Order   Cladida

(subgroup)   Ampelocrinida

Family   Calceolispongiidae

Size   Bottom of base about 5 centimeters wide

Time Period   Kungarian Stage of the Middle Permian, 273 to 283 million years ago

Location   Noonkanbah Formation, Mount Marmion, Western Australia.

Comments   The (Hinde's) Sponge Lily, *Calceolispongia hindei*, is one of several species of extinct sea lily echinoderms that lived in marine environments off the eastern coast of Pangaea that correspond to Western Australia and Timor.

When the sponge lily was originally discovered, it was thought to be a sponge. More fossils and more thorough examinations soon showed it to be an abberant crinoid, or sea lily, in that the basal plates of the cup, or body, are modified into blocks, so that the cup would have rested firmly on the seafloor like a five-legged tripod. The stalk, in turn, would have simply lain on the seafloor, rooted to the spot where the planktonic larva originally settled, trailing to the body almost like an electrical cord. It is thought that this was an adaptation to an environment filled with swift currents that would otherwise rip the crinoid off of its stalk.

The plates of *C. hindei* are decorated with a distinctive series of tubercles, and there is an immense amount of variation between individuals, even after taking erosion and damage before and after fossilization into account.

Name

Nevadan Snail Ammonite

Species *Cochloceras fischeri*

Phylum Mollusca

Class Cephalopoda

Subclass Ammonoidea

Order Ceratitida

Superfamily Clydonitaceae

Family Cochloceratidae

Size Shell height about 2 centimeters tall

Time Period Late Norian to Early Rhaetian epochs of the Late Triassic, 212 to 205 million years ago

Location *Cochloceras* Association, near Coaldale, Nevada

Comments The Nevadan Snail Ammonite, *Cochloceras fischeri*, is one of several American species of a wide-ranging genus of peculiar, tower-shaped ammonite that lived during the Late Triassic. Species of *Cochloceras* are used as index fossils for Late Triassic-aged marine strata, especially for those of the Norian and Rhaetian epochs. Fossils of the Nevadan snail ammonite, both empty and filled casts, and the original shells, are found in the *Cochloceras* Association, a limestone formation near the town of Coalsdale.

The Nevadan snail ammonite probably floated passively near the bottom of the sea floor, as the sculpture, shape and orientation of its shell would have, together, made swimming extremely difficult. The living animal may have snatched at suitable prey that blundered into range, picked up foraminiferan protists, or filter-fed.

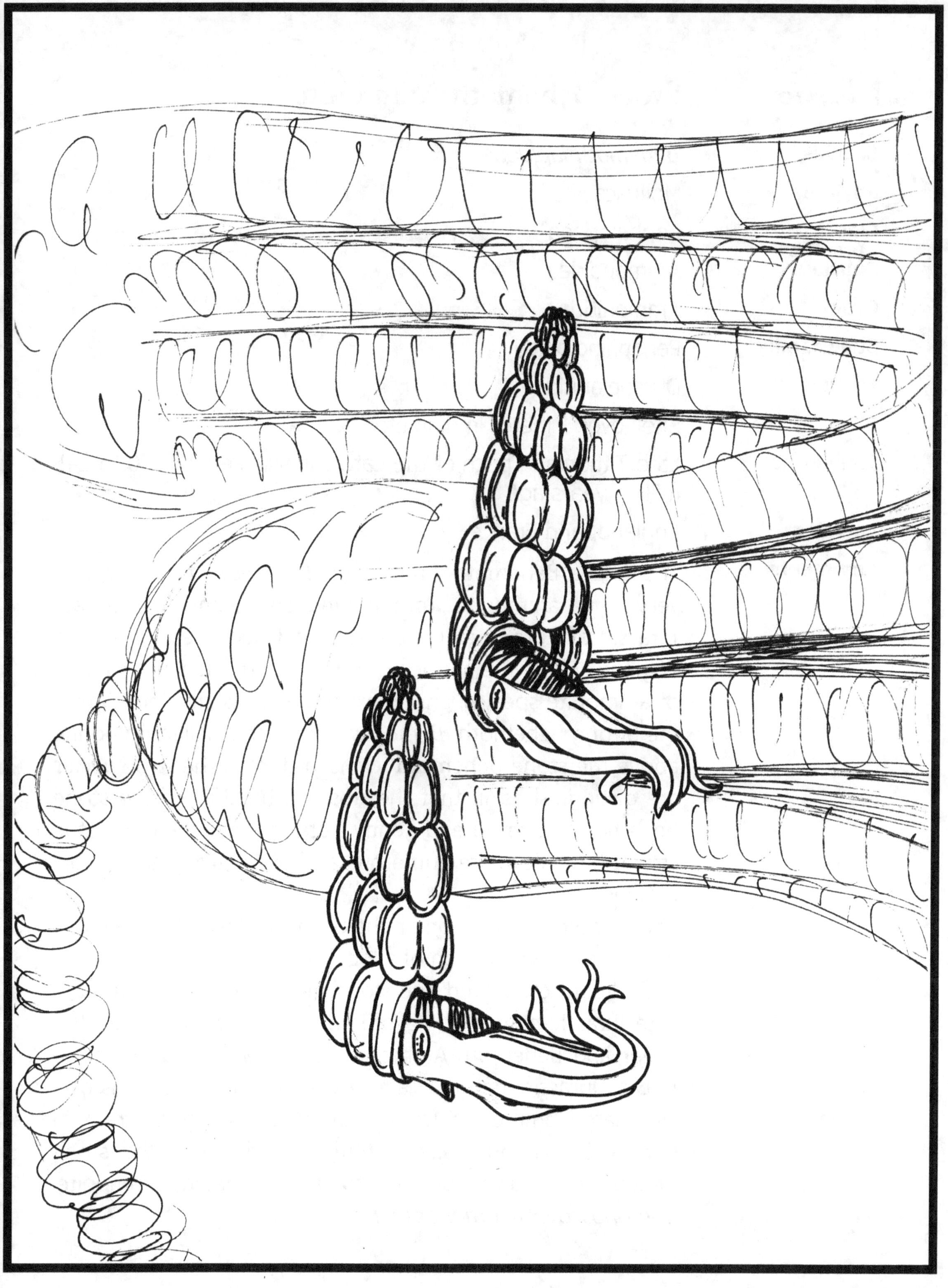

<table>
<tr><td>

Name

</td><td>

Stone Behemoth Ammonite

</td></tr>
<tr><td>**Species**</td><td>*Behemoth lapideus*</td></tr>
<tr><td>**Phylum**</td><td>Mollusca</td></tr>
<tr><td>**Class**</td><td>Cephalopoda</td></tr>
<tr><td>**Subclass**</td><td>Ammonoidea</td></tr>
<tr><td>**Order**</td><td>Ammonitida</td></tr>
<tr><td>**Superfamily**</td><td>Perisphinctoidea</td></tr>
<tr><td>**Family**</td><td>Dorsoplanitidae</td></tr>
<tr><td>**Size**</td><td>Shell over 1 meter in diameter</td></tr>
<tr><td>**Time Period**</td><td>Late Tithonian Epoch of the Late Jurassic Period, 150 to 145 million years ago</td></tr>
<tr><td>**Location**</td><td>England, and France</td></tr>
</table>

Comments

The Stone Behemoth Ammonite, *Behemoth lapideus*, is a very large ammonite from marine environments the Late Jurassic of Europe. The best-studied specimens are from England, where the species is found in a diverse assemblage of ammonite species, and coexisted with its smaller relative, the Strong Behemoth, *B. megasthene* (the smaller ammonite above the stone behemoth in the picture). The two species are distinguished in that the ribs on the shell of the stone behemoth are fewer and gently sloping, while the ribs of the strong behemoth are numerous and distinctively and boldly defined.

The holotype of the stone behemoth was taken from a block used in the construction of a local church.

In addition to England, the stone behemoth is also found in Late Jurassic marine strata of France. A related species, the Greenland Behemoth Ammonite, *B. groenlandicus,* is found in Late Jurassic marine strata of Greenland. Specimens of a very large ammonite from Late Jurassic marine strata in Central Russia originally identified as those of the stone behemoth actually belong to an unrelated ammonite, *Lomonossovella lomonossovi.*

<table>
<tr><td>

Name

</td><td>

Seppenrade Riesenammonite

</td></tr>
<tr><td>**Species**</td><td>*Parapuzosia seppenradensis*</td></tr>
<tr><td>**Class**</td><td>Cephalopoda</td></tr>
<tr><td>**Subclass**</td><td>Ammonoidea</td></tr>
<tr><td>**Order**</td><td>Ammonitida</td></tr>
<tr><td>**Superfamily**</td><td>Desmocerataceae</td></tr>
<tr><td>**Family**</td><td>Desmoceratidae</td></tr>
<tr><td>**Size**</td><td>Largest known specimen is an incomplete shell 180 centimeters in diameter, complete shell is estimated to be around 255 centimeters in diameter.</td></tr>
<tr><td>**Time Period**</td><td>Early Campanian epoch of the Late Cretaceous, about 80 million years ago</td></tr>
<tr><td>**Location**</td><td>Dulmen Beds, Westphalia, Germany.</td></tr>
<tr><td>**Comments**</td><td>

The Seppenrade Riesenammonite, *Parapuzosia seppenradensis*, is the largest ammonite known to humans, and is estimated to have weighed over a ton and a half, of which, half of that would have been the shell, estimated to have been over two and a half meters in diameter.

The Seppenrade riesenammonite lived what is now Westphalia, Northwestern Germany, about 80 million years ago, during the Campanian Epoch of the Late Cretaceous Period. As the specific name suggests, the holotype was found near the township of Seppenrade, which is near the city of Düsseldorf.

Ammonites of the genus *Parapuzosia* range in size from large to gigantic, and were found in oceans throughout the world. Here, the larger Seppenrade riesenammonite is compared to its slightly smaller French relative, Dabeer's Giant Ammonite, *P. dabeeri*, as they squabble over a fish carcass.

</td></tr>
</table>

Name

Chiapas Star Trumpetfish

Species	*Eekaulostomus cuevasae*
Phylum	Chordata
Superclass	Osteichthyes
Class	Actinopterygii
Order	Syngnathiformes
Superfamily	Aulostomoidea
Family	Eekaulostomidae
Size	A little over 8 centimeters
Time Period	Danian epoch of the Early Paleocene Period, 63 million years ago
Location	Belisario Domínguez quarry, Salto de Agua Municipality, Chiapas, Mexico (near Palenque)

Comments

The Chiapas Star Trumpetfish, *Eekaulostomus cuevasae*, is a syngnathiform fish closely related to both trumpetfishes (Family Aulostomoidae) and cornetfishes (Family Fistulariidae): the features of the Chiapas star trumpetfish demonstrate that it is either the last common ancestor of those two groups, or is very close to the last common ancestor of those two groups.

Of course, the Chiapas star trumpetfish differs drastically from either group; for example, the animal was covered in a series of star-shaped scutes referred to in its generic name ("Eek" being a Mayan word for star).

The living animal would have had a lifestyle very similar to pipefishes or modern aulostomoideans, being a slow-swimming stalker of smaller animals, which it vacuumed up with its mouth.

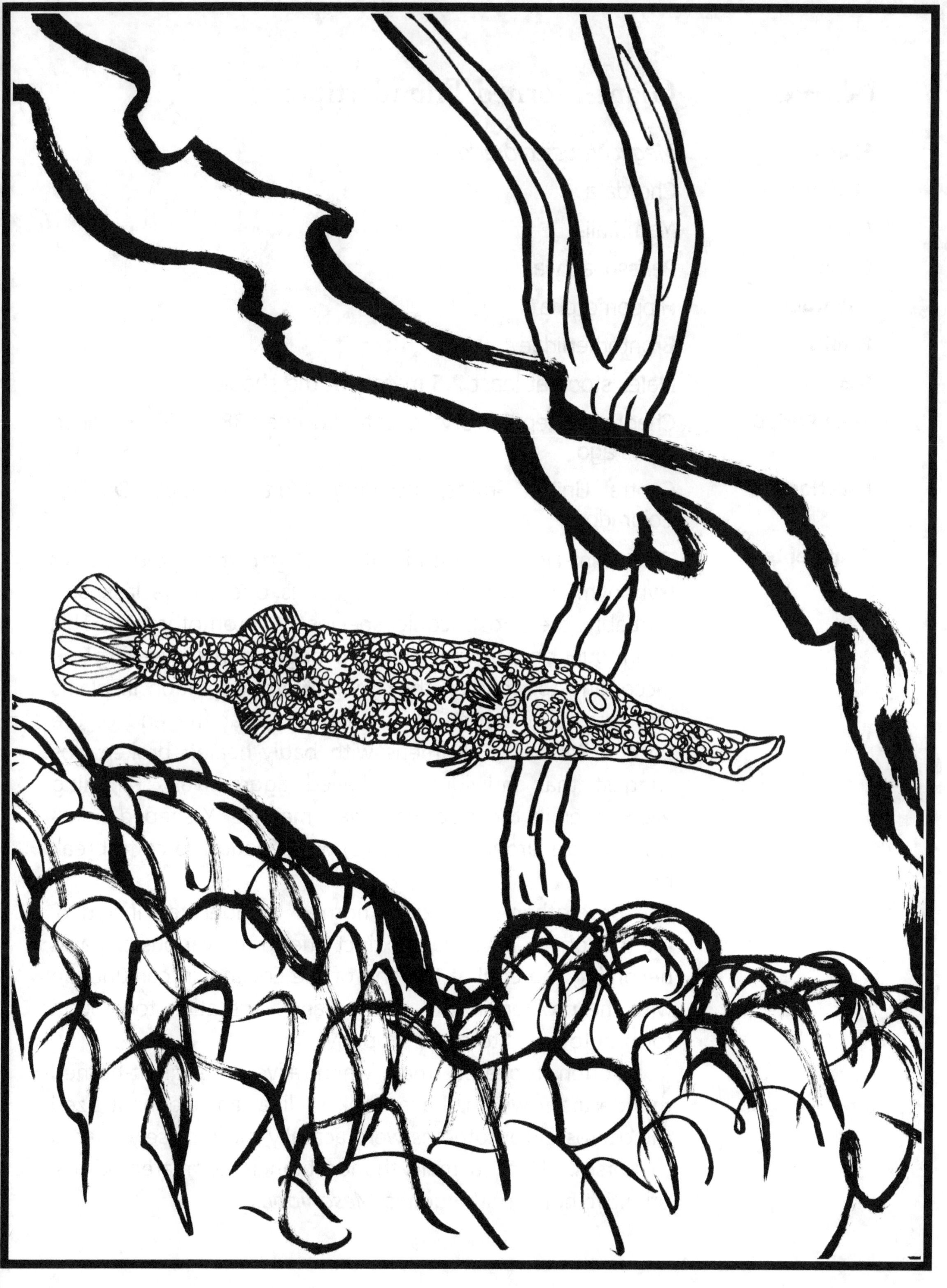

Name	Giant-Horned Thundertitan
Species	*Megacerops coloradensis*
Phylum	Chordata
Class	Mammalia
Order	Perissodactyla
Suborder	Hippomorpha
Family	Brontotheriidae
Size	Males stood at least 2.5 meters at the shoulders
Time Period	Chadronian epoch of the Late Eocene, 38 to 33.9 million years ago
Location	Central United States, including Nebraska, South Dakota, Colorado.
Comments	The Giant-Horned Thundertitan, *Megacerops coloradensis* (synonym = *Brontotherium gigas*), is one of the last, and probably the most iconic species of brontotheres. This enormous animal travelled in huge herds, feeding on (according to wear on their teeth) soft vegetation in plains and forests of central North America near the end of the Eocene Period. Specimens with badly-healed broken ribs suggest that individuals behaved aggressively, ramming each other in the side with their massive, Y-shaped horns (which were larger in the males) with enough force to break bones.

The brontotheres, the giant-horned thundertitan included, are thought to have went extinct due to the various climates becoming too cool at the end of the Eocene, in conjunction with the proliferation of grasses and vegetation too tough for brontotheres to chew properly.

It is often repeated that, when alive, the giant-horned thundertitan would have looked like an elephant-sized rhinoceros. Brontotheres were actually more closely related to horses. Here, a male thundertitan is compared with a primitive horse of the genus *Mesohippus*.

Name	Helohyid Peccary
Species	*Simojovelhyus pocitosense*
Phylum	Chordata
Class	Mammalia
Order	Artiodactyla
Family	Tayassuidae
Size	Very small, probably as large as a potbelly pig. Partial mandible about 5 centimeters long.
Time Period	Arikareean, or Rupelian Epoch of the Oligocene Period, 27 to 25 million years ago.
Location	An amber mine near Simojovel, Chiapas, Mexico, near the Guatemalan border.
Comments	The Helohyid Peccary, *Simojovelhyus pocitosense*, is a very small, primitive peccary from the Early Oligocene of Southern Mexico, and represents the oldest known fossil mammal from Central America.

When *S. pocitosense* was originally discovered and described in 2007, it was thought to be the youngest known helohyid, a variety of primitive artiodactyl related to hippopotamuses and anthracotheres that otherwise died out during the Middle Eocene. In 2013, paleontologist Donald Prothero and his associates published a paper refuting this, where they closely compared the holotype of *S. pocitosense* to helohyids and to Eocene and Oligocene-aged pecarries. The study noted the great similarities between peccaries and *S. pocitosense*, and comparatively fewer similarities between it and helohyids.

Name   Slingshot Deercamel

Species   *Synthetoceras tricornatus*

Phylum   Chordata

Class   Mammalia

Order   Artiodactyla

Infraorder   Tragulina

Family   Protoceratidae

Size   About 90 centimeters at the shoulder

Time Period   Early Serravellian to Late Messinian epochs of the Middle to Late Miocene, 13 to 5 million years ago

Location   Nebraska and Wyoming, United States

Comments   The Slingshot Deercamel, *Synthetoceras tricornatus*, is a peculiar-horned, deer or antelope-like relative of the chevrotains that lived in North America during the Miocene Period. The family Protoceratidae is an extinct group of artiodactyls that lived in North America from the Eocene until their extinction during the Pliocene. Protoceratids' placement in Artiodactyli has been in flux, having been placed in and moved from subgroup to subgroup for a little over a century. Recent anatomical comparisons place the group within Tragulina, a group that contains the chevrotains.

Both males and female slingshot deercamels had curved horns over their eye sockets, though, only the males had a long, slingshot-shaped horn, probably for intraspecific fights for territory and mating privileges. Here, a large male is compared with the giant camel, *Aepycamelus*.

Name

Beaked Whale Dolphin

Species	*Australodelphis mirus*
Phylum	Chordata
Class	Mammalia
Order	Artiodactyla
Infraorder	Cetacea
Family	Delphinidae
Size	Average skull length about 60 centimeters
Time Period	Middle Zanclean epoch of the Early Pliocene, about 4 million years ago
Location	Sørsdal Formation, Mule Peninsula, Vestfold Hills, East Antarctica.
Comments	The Beaked Whale Dolphin, *Australodelphis mirus*, is an extinct dolphin from what is now Eastern Antarctica that looked superficially very much like a beaked whale of the family Ziphiidae, albeit with an inverted mouth (in comparison to the jaws of true beaked whales). Unlike other delphinids (i.e., dolphins and killer whales), the beaked whale dolphin lacked any teeth in its jaws, and, could not capture prey by grasping with its jaws in a pincer-motion. Instead, anatomical evidence in the skulls of the animal suggest that prey was captured via suction through the toothless jaws, similar to the beaked whales of Ziphiidae. The factors surrounding the beaked whale dolphin's loss of teeth remain unknown, however.

Name	Giant Deer

Species — *Megaloceros giganteus*

Phylum — Chordata

Class — Mammalia

Order — Artiodactyla

Family — Cervidae

Size — Up to 210 centimeters at the shoulders, antlers' width around 360 centimeters across.

Time Period — Ionian Epoch of the Middle Pleistocene to the Holocene, from 780 thousand to 8 thousand years ago.

Location — Eurasia, from Ireland to Siberia and China.

Comments — The Giant Deer, *Megaloceros giganteus*, also known as the "Irish Elk," for how the best specimens come from Ice-Age bogs in Ireland, is one of the largest known deer species: its bodysize is matched by the Alaskan moose, *Alces alces gigas*. This massive beast stood a little over two meters at the shoulders, and males bore huge antlers spanning over 3 meters in width.

The giant deer was the last member of the megacerine deer, a diverse group of deer closely related to the fallow deer, *Dama sp.* The factors leading to the enormous antler-size, and to the giant deer's extinction have long been popular discussions among paleontologists for over two centuries. It appears obvious that the females' preference for large-antlered males drove the evolution of antlers so large that males would have been able to intimidate each other even without needing to fight with such awkward weapons. The cause of the giant deer's extinction is more murky. At first, it appears that the nutrient requirments to grow both big antlers and big calves drove the giant deer into extinction, until one notices that the last known individuals from Siberia did not appear to be suffering from nutritional deficiences and were developing normally, if only *slightly* smaller. Most likely, the giant deer's extinction was due to a number of complex factors, possibly even with separate populations dying out due to entirely different situations.

Name   Rodriguez Solitaire

Species	*Pezophas solitaria*
Phylum	Chordata
Class	Aves
Order	Columbiformes
Family	Columbidae
Subfamily	Raphinae
Size	Males up to 90 centimeters in height, females up to 70 centimeters height.
Time Period	Holocene, went extinct somewhere between the 1730's to 1760. Officially extinct by 1778AD.
Location	Rodriguez Island, in the Indian Ocean

Comments

The Rodriguez Solitaire, *Pezophaps solitaria*, is a very large, extinct pigeon that looked vaguely like a greyish brown swan. It was found in the forests of Rodriguez Island of the Mascarene Archipelago: its closest relative was the Dodo, *Raphus cucullatus*, of Mauritius, and its closest living relative is the Nicobar Pigeon, *Caloenas nicobarica*, Unlike the dodo, and most other pigeons, the solitaire lived alone, hence its name, or in mated pairs. French maroonee, François Leguat, made notes about the solitaires and other Rodriguez animals when he and his companions were shipwrecked on the island in 1691. Leguat is thought to be one of the few humans to observe and document the wildlife of that island. The paler, smaller female laid a single egg on a raised nest, and incubated it, then fed the chick crop-milk while while the male gathered fruits, seeds and leaves in his crop to feed his mate. The solitaire had a bony knob at the base of the wrist that was used to strike other solitaires during territorial fights. Leguat also noted that the solitaires beat their small wings to make noises to communicate with each other.

The Rodriguez solitaire went extinct partly due to tortoise-hunting sailors hunting them in addition to hunting the endemic giant tortoises, compounded with these same sailors destroying the forests and introducing dogs, cats, rats and monkeys that preyed on them and their chicks and eggs.

Bibliography

- Cantalice, Kleyton Magno, and Jesús Alvarado-Ortega. "Eekaulostomus cuevasae gen. and sp. nov., an ancient armored trumpetfish (Aulostomoidea) from Danian (Paleocene) marine deposits of Belisario Domínguez, Chiapas, southeastern Mexico." *Palaeontologia Electronica* 18.3 (2016): 1-24.
- Cheke, A. S.; Hume, J. P. (2008). Lost Land of the Dodo: an Ecological History of Mauritius, Réunion & Rodrigues. New Haven and London: T. & A. D. Poyser. ISBN 978-0-7136-6544-4.
- Evans, David H., and Andrew H. King. "Resolving polyphyly within the Endocerida: The Bisonocerida nov., a new order of early palaeozoic nautiloids." *Geobios* 45.1 (2012): 19-28.
- Fenton, Carroll Lane, et al. *The fossil book: a record of prehistoric life*. Courier Corporation, 1989.
- Flannery, Tim Fridtjof, and Peter Schouten. *A gap in nature: discovering the world's extinct animals*. Atlantic Monthly Press, 2001.
- Fordyce, R. Ewan, Patrick G. Quilty, and James Daniels. "Australodelphis mirus, a bizarre new toothless ziphiid-like fossil dolphin (Cetacea: Delphinidae) from the Pliocene of Vestfold Hills, East Antarctica." *Antarctic Science* 14.1 (2002): 37-54.
- Frickhinger, Karl Albert. *Fossil atlas, fishes*. Mergus, 1995.
- Fuller, Errol. "Extinct Birds (revised ed.)." *New York: Comstock* (2001): 33.
- Hess, Hans, and William I. Ausich. *Fossil crinoids*. Cambridge University Press, 2003.
- Kennedy, William James, and Ulrich Kaplan. *Parapuzosia (Parapuzosia) seppenradensis (Landois) und die Ammonitenfauna der Dülmener Schichten, unteres Unter-Campan, Westfalen*. Landschaftsverband Westfalen-Lippe, 1995.
- KOBAYASHI, Teiichi. "The Ordovician Palaeogeography of Eastern Asia." *Journal of Geography (Chigaku Zasshi)* 77.6 (1968): 313-328.
- Laws, Richard A. "Late Triassic depositional environments and molluscan associations from west-central Nevada." *Palaeogeography, Palaeoclimatology, Palaeoecology* 37.2-4 (1982): 131-148.
- Mitta, V. V. "THE SYSTEMATIC COMPOSITION OF THE MIDDLE VOLGIAN DORSOPLANITIDAE (AMMONOIDEA) FROM CENTRAL RUSSIA." *Paleontological Journal* 28 (1994): 1.
- Moore, Raymond Cecil, ed. *Treatise on Invertebrate Paleontology: Mollusca 3: Cepahalopoda--General Features--Endocertiodea--Actinoceratoidea--Nautilodea--Bactritoidea; by Curt Teichert...(et Al.).. Pt. K*. Geological Society of America, 1964.
- MULLER, SIEMON W., and Henry G. Ferguson. "Triassic and Lower Jurassic formations of west central Nevada." *Geological Society of America Bulletin* 47.2 (1936): 241-252.

- Nitecki, Matthew H., ed. *Mazon Creek Fossils*. Elsevier, 2013.
- Ou, Qiang, et al. "A vanished history of skeletonization in Cambrian comb jellies." *Science advances* 1.6 (2015): e1500092.
- Prothero, Donald R., and Scott E. Foss, eds. *The evolution of artiodactyls*. JHU Press, 2007.
- Prothero, Donald R., Brian L. Beatty, and Richard M. Stucky. "Simojovelhyus is a peccary, not a helohyid (Mammalia, Artiodactyla)." *Journal of Paleontology* 87.5 (2013): 930-933.
- Schram, Frederick R. "The Bear Gulch crustaceans and their bearing on late Paleozoic diversity and Permo-Triassic evolution of Malacostraca." *Compte rendu Neuvième Congrès International de Stratigraphie et de Géologie du Carbonifère*. Vol. 5. 1985.
- Schram, Frederick R. "Upper Pennsylvanian arthropods from black shales of Iowa and Nebraska." *Journal of Paleontology* (1984): 197-209.
- Stensiö, Erik A. "The Downtonian and Devonian vertebrates of Spitsbergen. I, Family Cephalaspidae." (1927).
- Teichert, Curt. "Permian crinoid Calceolispongia." *Geological Society of America Memoirs* 34 (1949): 1-155.
- Townson, W. G., and W. A. Wimbledon. "The Portlandian strata of the Bas Boulonnais, France." *Proceedings of the Geologists' Association* 90.1-2 (1979): 81-91.
- Turner, Alan. *National Geographic Prehistoric Mammals*. National Geographic, 2004.
- Webster, G. D., and P. A. Jell. "New Permian crinoids from Australia." *MEMOIRS-QUEENSLAND MUSEUM* 43.1 (1999): 279-339.
- Wittry, Jack. *The Mazon Creek Fossil Fauna*. Esconi, 2012.
- Wright, C. W., J. H. Callomon, and M. K. Howarth. "Cretaceous Ammonoidea. Volume 4. Mollusca 4. Revised." *Treatise on Invertebrate Paleontology. NY: Univ. Kansas Press*. 1996. 362.
- Xian-Guang, Hou, et al. *The Cambrian fossils of Chengjiang, China: the flowering of early animal life*. John Wiley & Sons, 2017.

About the Artist

Stanton F. Fink is a student of Biology and Chinese Medicine, and makes a hobby of drawing monsters and researching flowers, arcane-looking creatures, prehistoric animals, fish, reptiles, birds and the occasional, really grotesque fungal fruiting body.

Stanton grew up and went to school in California and is currently living, drawing, and gardening in Oregon.